MONEY GROWS WHERE YOU PLANT IT

By

Samson Osunkojo

MONEY GROWS WHERE YOU PLANT IT

Dedication

To God Almighty for His grace upon my life.

And to the loving memory of my late brother, Olusoji Osunkojo.

Acknowledgement

I acknowledge the Maker of men who has been my strength and help since the ages.

I also sincerely appreciate my parents, Pastor & Pastor Mrs. Amos Osunkojo, for the path of righteousness they have shown us.

I appreciate my darling wife, Opeyemi Osunkojo, and our beautiful children for their support in making this book a reality.

My humble appreciation goes to my brother, *Chief Saheed Oladele (Baameko of Ibadan Land), founder of Erudite Millennium Limited, for the valuable time you devoted to writing the foreword of this book despite your busy schedule. I don't take this for granted, thank you, sir.*

My appreciation also goes to Segun Ajisekola for his efforts in making this book a success. Thank you, Dr. Akeem Bakare, for your effort and time in editing the book. Much appreciation, also, to my friend Muyiwa Ogunyemi for the fantastic design of the book.

I acknowledge the support of my Pastor (Pastor James Kayode Olusoji) for his valuable input toward the book's reality. I am a product of grace, so I must appreciate all my spiritual fathers, mothers, and mentors.

I also acknowledge Book Writing League's support in helping bring this book to the masses.

God bless you all!

Disclaimer

This book is not intended to be used as a source of investment advice with any organization. All readers are advised to consult and seek all necessary legal, business, and financial advice before investing in or engaging in any industry.

The author does not assume any responsibility or liability whatsoever for what you choose to do with the information about people or organizations you read in the book.

Table of Contents

Foreword

It is often said that education is the seedbed of transformation. In every generation, select voices arise that awaken others to see possibilities where they once saw limitations. *Money Grows Where You Plant It* is, therefore, one such voice, a book that is clear, practical, and deeply rooted in wisdom.

As an educator, I have learned that authentic learning goes beyond the classroom walls. It is about re-educating the mind to think differently, act intentionally, and create value from within. This book does precisely that. It challenges the myths we have been taught about money, strips away the illusions of luck and chance, and presents wealth for what it truly is: a harvest born of purposeful planting.

Samson Osunkojo has written not just a financial guide, but a life manual. With remarkable clarity, he connects age-old principles of diligence, vision, and service to modern realities of entrepreneurship, investment, and personal growth. His approach is particularly refreshing because it is rooted in both faith and practicality, ambition and responsibility.

Therefore, for young professionals seeking direction, entrepreneurs searching for depth, and everyday people simply seeking to break free from financial struggle, this book is a timely compass. It teaches that wealth creation is not reserved for a few but is attainable for all who are willing to plant wisely, water patiently, and grow consistently.

As I read through its pages, I was reminded that education is not complete until it empowers. And this book, in every sense, enables the reader's mind, heart, and habit.

Therefore, I wholeheartedly recommend *Money Grows Where You Plant It* to every reader who desires not just to earn money but to understand it, multiply it, and use it for good.

May the seeds planted through this book yield abundance in your life and in future generations.

Chief Saheed Oladele

Baameko of Ibadan Land

Preface

This book was born out of countless conversations, quiet reflections, and lived experiences that revealed a truth many of us overlook: **wealth does not simply happen; it grows where we choose to plant it.**

Over the years, I have met people from all walks of life — dreamers, hustlers, entrepreneurs, and even those who have lost hope in ever achieving financial freedom. What struck me most was not their lack of effort or intelligence but a profound misunderstanding of what it truly takes to build lasting wealth.

Therefore, I wrote this book not as a financial manual filled with numbers and jargon, but as a guide to shift the way you see money. Here, we explore how mindset, emotional intelligence, intentional action, and purpose-driven entrepreneurship can transform not only your finances but also your life.

This is not a book of quick fixes or lottery-like promises. It is a journey, a seed planted in fertile ground. If you nurture these principles with patience and courage, you will find that success is not a distant dream. It is already in your hands, waiting to grow.

Introduction

Money often feels mysterious, like something that some are "lucky" to have while others struggle endlessly to attain. But in truth, money is neither luck nor magic; it is a seed.

Just like gardeners carefully select where to sow seeds for the richest harvest, the way we think, invest, and serve determines the wealth we create. Most of us nurture the anecdotal belief that wealth is a finite pie, where someone else's gain must mean our loss. But the reality is far more abundant: **true wealth expands when we plant, water, and cultivate it with intention.**

In this book, you will discover:

- ❖ Why hard work alone won't make you rich, and what truly creates prosperity.

- ❖ How money responds to our mindset shifts, values, and energy.

- ❖ Practical ways to invest your time, skills, and other resources for lasting financial growth.

- ❖ The role of services that create impact, purpose that drives vision, and entrepreneurship that engenders wealth.

- ❖ How to break free from your primordial money myths and other emotional blocks that hold you back from becoming wealthy.

Ultimately, this book is an invitation to think differently, act intentionally, and build wealth in a way that not only fills your pockets but also enriches your life and those around you.

"Plant the right seeds, nurture them well, and watch as your life transforms from the ground up."

— Samson Osunkojo

Chapter 1

Why Wealth Isn't a Zero-Sum Game

For generations, we have been taught to view wealth as a pie, finite, limited, and fiercely divided. If someone takes a bigger slice, there's automatically less for everyone else. Economists call this a zero-sum mindset, and it is deeply ingrained. Unfortunately, it has quietly held many people back from stepping into absolute abundance.

But here's the truth: wealth, true lasting wealth, is not a pie at all. It is more like a **garden**. With care, intention, and consistency, it grows. It multiplies. And the best part? There's room for everyone to plant, cultivate, and reap the harvest.

The Scarcity Myth

From an early age, we are taught to internalize beliefs like:

- ❖ "Money does not grow on trees."
- ❖ "The rich get richer while the poor stay poor."
- ❖ "If I do not take it first, someone else will."

These phrases become the silent scripts many of us live by; scripts rooted more in fear than in truth. But here's the reality: **wealth expands when value is created**.

In microeconomics, we talk about **opportunity costs**, the costs you incur by choosing one option over another. If money just sits idle in a savings account while inflation rises, it loses purchasing power. But if planted in the "right soil," a business, a powerful idea, a skill, or even a meaningful relationship, it grows.

Your effort is the seed. Your belief is the sunlight. Consistency is the water.

The Expansion of Wealth

Wealth is not discovered. It is created. Through **innovation, entrepreneurship, and productivity**, we generate wealth that did not exist before. This is what macroeconomists call **positive-sum growth**, where everyone can win.

Consider this:

- ❖ Before online platforms gave Nigerian artists a global stage, their markets were limited to local buyers. Today, with Spotify, AudioMarck, or iTunes, they attract foreign Income, contributing to Nigeria's economy.

- ❖ Before sellers could market on Instagram or TikTok, or Jumia, that income stream did not exist.

- ❖ Before writers began self-publishing on Amazon Kindle or OkadaBooks, their words had no paying audience beyond their neighborhood.

Wealth is not about taking from someone else; rather, it is about creating something new, born from imagination, courage, and purposeful action.

A tale of two friends, Ayo and David

Ayo and David grew up in the same neighborhood, both from humble beginnings. One day, each of them received a ₦1,000 gift from a local mentorship program.

David thought, *"That's not enough to do anything meaningful."* So he placed it in a savings account and waited.

Ayo, on the other hand, invested ₦1,000 in an online graphic design course. She practiced relentlessly, failing, adjusting, and improving.

Six months later, she landed her first client. Then another. Soon, she was earning ₦2,000 a month doing what she loved.

David shook his head and said, *"She just got lucky."* But it wasn't just luck. It was **human capital investment**; money turned into knowledge and knowledge turned into Income.

While David's money sat idle, quietly eroded by inflation, Ayo's money multiplied. That's the power of planting wisely.

Wealth Is Energy

Money is more than currency; it is energy, and like all kinds of energy, it seeks flow and order. In economics, capital gravitates toward value, just as systems organize themselves to resist entropy. Investors channel funds into ideas and businesses that generate returns, but without continuous creation and renewal, that energy disperses, opportunities decay, and entropy wins.

If you see money as scarce, you may hoard it or chase it with desperation. But if you see it as abundant, you attract it by solving problems and creating genuine value for others.

Hence, the challenge is not only external but internal. Personal growth, emotional healing, and self-awareness are essential for building lasting wealth. You cannot pour value into your business or clients if you are operating from a place of fear or insecurity.

Summarily, money flows where energy goes. If you fixate on what you lack, you will feel that lack more deeply. But when you focus your energy on value creation, wealth eventually reflects that effort.

Planting in the Right Soil of Life

Remember, planting is not limited to business ventures. It can also mean:

- ❖ Investing in your marriage to create a peaceful home.
- ❖ Focusing on education to gain skills that open doors, which economists call **increasing your marginal productivity**.
- ❖ Healing old wounds so you stop self-sabotaging.
- ❖ Building community connections that translate into social and financial capital.

The people you admire didn't stumble into wealth by chance. They planted strategically, nurtured patiently, and harvested consistently.

Emotional Intelligence: A Hidden Currency

Think about it. What happens when a business owner loses their cool with a client? Or when an employee cannot handle feedback? Or when a partner shuts down during conflict? These emotional barriers eventually cost money.

In business, we'd call this an **increase in transaction costs**; frictions that make business less efficient. Emotional intelligence reduces those costs.

Emotional intelligence is the ability to recognize and manage your own emotions while understanding and influencing others' emotions. It helps you:

- ❖ Build stronger, cohesive teams
- ❖ Navigate difficult negotiations
- ❖ Stay calm in crises
- ❖ Make clear, confident decisions

The more emotionally intelligent you become, the better you are at attracting wealth and keeping it.

Personal Growth Is the Ultimate Wealth Strategy

Wealth is not really about what sits in your bank account. It starts in your head. **Human capital, skills, discipline, and mindset are the ultimate drivers of prosperity.**

Confidence, discipline, and emotional maturity are the true currencies behind lasting wealth. Money naturally flows to those mature enough to grow it.

Closing Thought

Wealth is not a pie to be divided. It is a garden waiting to be cultivated. The real question is not whether wealth can grow, but whether you are ready to grow with it.

Chapter 2

Hard Work vs. Smart Work: Why Effort Alone Won't Make You Rich

We have all heard the saying: *"Just work hard, and you will succeed."*

It is repeated in classrooms, from the pulpit, and even around family dinner tables. While the advice sounds noble and is often meant to inspire, it only tells half the story.

If hard work alone guaranteed wealth, then farmers, janitors, and factory workers, the backbone of our economy, would be the wealthiest among us. But they aren't. And that reveals a more profound truth: **effort without leverage rarely leads to prosperity**.

The Myth of Hard Work Alone

In many cultures, especially in Nigeria, hard work is almost worshipped. Hustling is worn like a badge of honor. We glorify the "all-nighter," the endless grind, the sleepless pursuit of survival.

But here's the problem: without **strategy, systems, and leverage**, hard work can trap you in a cycle of exhaustion without progress. In Economics, this is called **diminishing returns**: putting in more effort yields less with each additional unit of effort.

Think about it:

- ❖ You can work 16-hour days and still struggle to pay bills.
- ❖ You can juggle two jobs abroad and still send money home with nothing left to save.
- ❖ You can pour your energy into building someone else's dream and never create your own.

Hard work keeps you busy. Clever work delivers results.

The Shift: From Labor to Leverage

So, what separates those who grind endlessly from those who earn more while working less? The answer is **leverage**.

Leverage means using tools, systems, and people to **multiply output without multiplying effort**. It is the principle that separates survival earners from wealth creators. So, what kinds of leverage are there? Here, we discuss time, systems, people, and money leverage.

1. Time Leverage

We all have 24 hours a day. No one gets extra. But competent workers stretch time through delegation, automation, and scalable models.

Example: A Nigerian freelance writer who creates an online course has stopped trading time for money. That course generates passive Income even while they sleep. This is what economists call **breaking the time-income correlation**.

2. System Leverage

Systems are repeatable processes that reduce waste and improve efficiency.

Think of an online store owner who automates order fulfillment and email marketing. Instead of chasing every sale, the system keeps revenue flowing while they focus on growth.

In business economics, this is called **increasing productivity per unit of effort**.

3. People Leverage

Investing in people is one of the most powerful multipliers. Your network, mentors, collaborators, clients, and communities can create opportunities that no amount of individual hustle can.

Economists call this **social capital**. In business, we call it partnerships. In Nigeria, we say, *"Your network is your net worth."*

A coach who trains other coaches scales her Income without adding hours. An entrepreneur with a strong diaspora network can access investors and suppliers faster than someone working alone.

4. Money Leverage

Finally, wealthy people do not hustle for every naira. They let their money work for them. Investments in stocks, real estate, or small businesses create passive Income and expand assets.

This is **capital leverage**. In macroeconomics, nations grow when capital is deployed into productive ventures. On a personal scale, individuals develop the same way.

People Are Multipliers, Not Just Resources

Smart people do not just grind harder. They plant seeds in the right places, especially in people.

- ❖ A strong network can open doors faster than raw effort.
- ❖ Relationships built on trust are compounded like interests.
- ❖ Communities provide support, opportunities, and referrals that cannot be bought.

Every connection is a seed. How you nurture it determines what it becomes: a partnership, a collaboration, or a bridge to your next opportunity. Your emotional intelligence comes in handy here, helping you build and maintain connections.

Relational Wealth: The Story of Malik

Malik grew up in a low-income neighborhood with limited options. But he had one strength: relationships. He remembered names, followed up on conversations, and genuinely wanted others to succeed.

When he launched his sneaker business, he had no investors. But his network, friends, mentors, and coworkers became his first customers, advisors, and ambassadors. Years later, he sold his brand to a major retailer.

People said he was "lucky." But it wasn't luck; instead, it was years of planting seeds in people. We can, therefore, conclude that his connections were his startup capital.

Healing the Wounds That Block Connection

For some, networking does not come easily. Betrayal, rejection, or cultural mistrust makes us hesitant to open up. But in business, closed networks limit opportunities, while open ones create spillover effects.

Competent wealth builders learn to heal, rebuild trust, and lean into connection. Vulnerability often opens the doors that talent alone cannot.

Real Story: From Burnout to Breakthrough

Chidera was a single mother juggling two jobs. Exhausted, broke, and constantly behind on bills, she stumbled across a book titled 'The 4-Hour Work Week'. The book sparked an idea: *"Maybe I do not need to work harder. Maybe I need to work smarter."*

She began learning digital skills in the evenings: web design, branding, and email marketing. Within two years, she was running a small agency, working fewer hours, earning four times more, and spending weekends with her kids.

Chidera didn't stop working hard. She redirected her energy with **strategy and leverage**. Here, she leveraged systems and time.

The Trap of Trading Time for Money

When you only trade hours for money, your Income is capped. You are bound by:

- ❖ Your boss's decisions
- ❖ Your physical energy
- ❖ The relentless ticking of the clock

However, absolute freedom begins when you build **assets and income streams** that do not depend solely on your time. This does not mean quitting your job overnight. It means planting seeds that grow beyond your immediate labor. Like someone once said, hard work pays, but only minimum wage.

Closing Thought

Hard work is honorable, but by itself, it is not enough. Wealth comes from working smart, leveraging time, systems, people, and money to create more value than one person could ever produce alone.

Chapter 3

Money as a Seed: Where You Plant It Determines Growth

Money as a Seed

Money often gets a bad reputation. People idolize it, fear it, chase it, or resent it.

But have you ever paused to ask yourself: *What is money, really?*

At its core, money is simply a **medium of exchange**, a practical tool we use to assign value and facilitate trade. But from another angle, money is also like a **seed**. Just like any seed, its growth rate depends entirely on where, how, and why you choose to plant it.

The Cost of Doing Nothing with Money: Inflation and Lost Potential Returns

Imagine this: you have a bag of seeds, but instead of planting them, you toss them in a cupboard and forget about them. Over time, they dry out, lose vitality, and eventually become useless.

That is precisely what happens to money when it sits idle.

In a world of constant inflation, the longer your cash sits untouched, the more its value quietly erodes. Inflation, simply put, is the gradual, general rise in price levels over time. It may not seem dramatic day to day, but over the years, its impact has been enormous.

For example, that ₦100,000 you saved five years ago might today only buy goods worth ₦40,000 or less. The money did not vanish, but its **purchasing power** shrank.

This is why letting money sit without a purpose is costly. In fact, macroeconomists warn that economies stagnate when too much capital is left unproductive. On the personal level, idle money is just wasted potential.

Just like seeds need soil to grow, money needs to be **put to work**. If it sits dormant, it loses potential. But when planted wisely, it can multiply and create a lasting impact.

Planting the Seed: The Power of Strategic Investment

To truly grow your money, you need to place it where it can thrive. This is not just about spending less or saving more. It is about **investing with intention and strategy**.

Here are a few key principles:

1. Compounding Interest

Compounding is one of the most powerful forces in finance. It means you earn Interest not only on your original investment but also on the Interest that accumulates over time. This creates a ripple effect of growth.

For example, in economics and statistics, there is something called the rule of 72. That is, if your asset (money) earns 1% interest every month, its value will double in just 72 months.

Take Kemi, for example: she begins investing $100 a month at age 25 in a diversified index fund with an average annual return of 8%. By age 55 (30 years after her first contribution), her investments have grown far beyond her total contributions (17.45x). Her investments will have grown to over $135,000, even though she only contributed $36,000 out of pocket.

Compounding is your reward for **consistency and patience**. It turns small, steady efforts into life-changing results.

2. Reinvesting Profits

Another essential principle is reinvesting profits. When your investments pay off—through dividends, business income, or rental returns- it is tempting to cash out and celebrate. But the more brilliant move is to **reinvest**.

Think of it this way: when you harvest fruit from a tree, you plant the seeds again. Over time, what began as one tree becomes a forest. Economists call this the **accumulation effect**. Reinvested capital fuels faster growth than consumption ever could.

3. Asset Accumulation

Assets are anything that consistently puts money in your pocket. They include real estate, stocks, intellectual property, or businesses.

Accumulating assets is like planting crops that yield harvest after harvest. They do not just grow in value; they also continue to generate Income.

Take Tunde, for example. He started a small graphic design business, invested in better equipment, studied marketing, and built a reliable team. Five years later, his business runs smoothly with minimal daily involvement and generates steady cash flow. Tunde's skills became an **asset**, and that asset now pays him.

Choosing Fertile Ground: Where to Plant Your Money

Now that we have talked about how to plant, let's explore **where to plant**. Not every opportunity is fertile soil, and not every investment will bear fruit. But there are proven, productive places:

A. STOCK MARKET AND INDEX FUNDS

The stock market, primarily through index funds, is a strong long-term wealth builder. When you buy stocks, you buy ownership in businesses, and businesses create value.

Yes, markets go up and down, but historically they rise over time. The key is to diversify, stay consistent, and think long-term.

For example, the Nigerian Stock Exchange All-Share Index (NGX-ASI) has grown at an annual rate of 7.6% over the past 20 years. Similarly, the S&P 500 of the New York Stock Exchange and NASDAQ in the US have grown at 9.8% annually over the past 20 years.

B. REAL ESTATE

Real estate has always been one of the surest ways to build wealth that lasts. For generations, property has been the backbone of stability and legacy. With the right mindset and patience, it appreciates steadily, even when the economy feels shaky.

Think about it: land rarely loses value. It keeps rising, and it can outlive you. Property is tangible; you can walk on it, live on it, pass it down to your children, and even expand your holdings with time. Buying land or property, therefore, is more than an investment. It is planting a seed of potential that grows year after year.

As Will Rogers once said, *"Don't wait to buy real estate. Buy real estate and wait."*

Picture yourself standing in an empty field. To the casual eye, it looks like just dirt and silence. But to someone with vision, that land is bursting with possibilities. Real estate is not only about bricks and blocks; rather, it is about foresight, faith, and turning raw potential into lasting wealth.

When you make intentional choices that align with your goals, property becomes one of the richest grounds to plant your money. And just like any seed, it must be grown, nurtured, and harvested with wisdom. That wisdom does not start with cash. It starts with mindset.

THE EMOTIONAL VALUE OF OWNING GROUND

Owning property is more than financial rewards; it is also an emotional experience. For many families who were denied land in the past, finally holding a piece of earth is healing. It is taking back power and rewriting your family story.

When you own land or a house, you are not just building equity; you are creating a sense of belonging and stability for the next generation. Watching a property rise in value, seeing tenants thrive in a home you built, or standing on land you once dreamed of—that's bigger than money. That is legacy.

Why Real Estate? Why Now?

- ❖ **It is tangible**: Unlike stocks or crypto, property is physical. You can use it, improve it, rent it, or sell it.

- ❖ **It appreciates**: Properties usually increase in value, especially in fast-growing areas.

- ❖ **It generates passive Income**: Rentals bring in steady money while you sleep.

- ❖ **It allows leverage**: With mortgages or partnerships, you can control bigger assets using other people's money.

- ❖ **It builds legacy**: Property can be passed down, giving your children a head start.

The truth is simple: real estate rewards those who think long-term. It is not about a quick flip. It is about planting seeds and letting them grow into a forest of stability and wealth.

Types of Real Estate Ventures

Each real estate path is like a seed, with its own timeline and rewards.

1. Land Banking: The Silent Wealth Builder

Mark Twain once said, *"Buy land. They're not making it anymore."*

What it is: Land banking is buying undeveloped land in areas that will grow in value.

How it works: You buy land cheaply, often at the edge of town. As development pushes outwards, roads, schools, and shopping centers, the land appreciates. You can later sell it for profit or build on it.

Emotional takeaway: Land banking is an act of vision and patience. The returns do not come overnight, but they can change your life.

Case Study: Tasha's Story

Tasha, a single mom in Georgia, used her tax refund to buy three acres of rural land. People mocked her "empty" plot. A decade later, her land sat between two booming subdivisions. She sold it ten times the initial price and paid off her mortgage. That's the power of patience.

2. Rental Properties: Passive Income, Active Impact

What it is: You buy a property, maybe a house, duplex, or apartment, and rent it out for Income.

How it works: The rent covers your mortgage, taxes, and often leaves a profit. Meanwhile, the property itself gains value. You win twice: monthly cash flow and long-term equity.

Types to consider

- ❖ **Long-term rentals**: Families or professionals on 6–12-month leases.
- ❖ **Short-term rentals**: Airbnb or Vrbo for tourists and business travelers.

Emotional takeaway: Being a landlord is not just about collecting rent. It is about responsibility. You are providing shelter, one of life's most basic and powerful needs.

C. AGRICULTURE

Farming may look old-fashioned to some, but it is timeless. Agriculture has always been the backbone of civilizations, and it remains one of the most underestimated paths to wealth today. In a world where food insecurity is rising and populations keep expanding, agriculture has become more profitable than ever.

A backyard poultry pen or a cassava field that seems small today can grow into a multi-million-naira agribusiness tomorrow. Beyond the financial rewards, agriculture teaches qualities that every wealth builder needs: patience, resilience, and stewardship.

Agriculture: A Path to Purpose and Profit

There is something sacred about placing a seed in the ground and waiting for it to rise. You cannot force it, nor rush it. You can water, protect, and believe, but the miracle of growth belongs to time.

Farming is one of the clearest metaphors for generational wealth. It connects us to the earth, grounds us in patience, and reveals the discipline of nurturing what cannot be seen immediately. When pursued with vision and wisdom, farming is not just profitable; it is also fulfilling. It is also healing.

As Masanobu Fukuoka once said: *"The ultimate goal of farming is not the growing of crops, but the cultivation and perfection of human beings."*

In a world obsessed with quick money, farming quietly reminds us that some things grow slowly but surely.

Agriculture: The Foundation of Civilizations

Long before there were stocks, skyscrapers, or software, there was land. For centuries, agriculture sustained families, cultures, and economies.

Even now, it is often underestimated. Many people see only dirt, sweat, and unpredictability. But when approached strategically, agriculture becomes one of the most stable and abundant wealth-building tools available.

In today's reality of food shortages, population booms, and climate challenges, those who learn how to nurture the earth are not just ensuring survival. They are building financial freedom.

Two Pillars of Agricultural Wealth

1. Crop Farming: Cultivating Abundance from the Ground Up

What it is: Crop farming is the practice of growing plants for food, fiber, or fuel. From grains like rice, corn, and wheat to vegetables, legumes, and specialty herbs, this form of farming turns soil into both sustenance and steady cash flow.

Types of crop farming

- ❖ Subsistence farming focuses on small-scale production to feed households or communities.

- ❖ Commercial farming involves larger-scale operations focused on profit, often using tractors, irrigation, and supply chains.

- ❖ Organic farming uses natural methods to grow crops without synthetic pesticides or GMOs and thrives in health-conscious markets.

- ❖ High-value crops such as ginger, turmeric, strawberries, and mushrooms fetch premium prices locally and globally.

How it builds wealth

- ❖ Generates consistent Income through seasonal harvests.

- ❖ Offers scalability, as a small farm can grow when profits are reinvested.

- ❖ Provides export potential, especially in fertile regions.

- ❖ Requires low entry capital since even a backyard garden can generate Income.

Emotional lesson: Crop farming teaches timing and trust. You must plant early, work consistently, and believe in the invisible processes happening underground. The most meaningful growth often remains hidden until harvest.

Case Study: Sarah's Acre

Sarah, a widow in Uganda, started with just one acre of cassava. Everyone doubted her. But she worked on the land faithfully, later adding tomatoes, okra, and maize. Five years later, she was supplying hotels, employing widows, and paying for her children's education. The soil beneath her feet became her lifeline.

2. Livestock Farming: Breeding Life That Sustains Life

What it is: livestock farming is the raising of animals for food, fiber, or other products. This includes cows, goats, pigs, chickens, sheep, and even fish.

Types of livestock businesses

- ❖ Poultry farming involves raising chickens or turkeys for meat and eggs. It has high demand and quick turnover.

- ❖ Cattle rearing provides beef or dairy. It is a long-term investment with high resale value.

- ❖ Goat and sheep farming is easier to manage on smaller land and provides both meat and milk.

- ❖ Pig farming offers high reproduction rates and strong profit potential when managed well.

- ❖ Fish farming, or aquaculture, involves breeding fish such as tilapia or catfish in ponds or tanks.

How it builds wealth:

- ❖ It creates multiple income streams through meat, eggs, milk, hides, and even manure used as fertilizer.

- ❖ Produces quick returns, especially with poultry or piglets, within 4 to 6 months.

- ❖ Meets consistent demand because people will always need food.

- ❖ Opens opportunities across the value chain in feed production, veterinary services, processing, and packaging.

Emotional lesson:

Livestock teaches rhythm and responsibility. Animals are not machines. They require care, attention, and consistency. When they thrive, you thrive.

Case Study: Babatunde's Backyard Breakthrough

Babatunde, a teacher in Nigeria, started a small backyard poultry farm with just 20 chickens, a notebook, and a dream. Every evening after school, he fed them, tracked their growth, and reinvested every naira he earned. Today, he supplies eggs across three states and employs ten people. His legacy did not start with a contract. It started from his backyard.

Beyond Farming: Exploring the Agricultural Ecosystem

Agriculture is not limited to digging or planting. It offers many other paths to wealth through the ecosystem that surrounds it.

- ❖ Agro-processing transforms raw produce into higher-value goods, such as turning cassava into flour, tomatoes into paste, or mangoes into juice.

- ❖ Storage and logistics businesses offer warehouse or cold storage solutions to reduce spoilage and waste.

- ❖ Agritech introduces drones, mobile apps, or innovative irrigation systems to boost productivity.

- ❖ Agro-education focuses on teaching farming skills, whether online, in classrooms, or through hands-on workshops.

- ❖ Agro-finance provides loans, insurance, or crowdfunding platforms designed for farmers.

You do not need fifty acres to succeed. You only need vision and a clear sense of where you can add value.

The Inner Harvest: What Farming Teaches the Soul

Agriculture does more than build financial wealth. It nurtures emotional, mental, and spiritual growth.

- ❖ It teaches patience in a world obsessed with instant results. You wait for rain, for germination, and for harvest.

- ❖ It teaches faith because you cannot see the roots growing, but you believe they are.

- ❖ It teaches resilience because floods and pests will come, but breakthroughs will also come.

- ❖ It teaches stewardship, reminding us to respect both the earth and ourselves.

Overcoming Barriers: Healing Our Fear of the Soil

For many, farming brings memories of hardship or "village life." They say, "My parents suffered on the farm. I want better." But perhaps it is better not to escape the soil. Possibly better is redeeming it.

Your parents may have farmed with cutlasses. You can farm with drones. They carried yams in baskets. You can sell online and in bulk. They lived from season to season. You can thrive from one strategy to the next.

Farming is not backward. It is forward when you choose to see it differently.

Planting Questions: Is Agriculture My Next Seed?

- ❖ What skills or resources do I already have?
- ❖ Do I enjoy working with the earth, animals, or natural cycles?
- ❖ What farming model fits my time, budget, and lifestyle?
- ❖ Can I partner with others to start small?
- ❖ What products are in demand in my local or regional market?
- ❖ Am I ready to commit to patient, steady growth?

Farming is not a lottery. It is a lifestyle.

From Dirt to Destiny

Money truly grows where you plant it. And there is no place more literal, more sacred, or more poetic to plant than the soil beneath your feet.

Agriculture reminds us that wealth does not always shout from skyscrapers. Sometimes it whispers through seeds, sings in harvests, and lives in animals that nourish families. It shows up in hands marked by labor and hearts driven by purpose.

D. SERVICE: TURNING SKILLS INTO SEEDS OF WEALTH

Service is not just about getting by. It is about making a difference. There comes a moment when you realize that what you hold in your hands, what you know, love, and do effortlessly, can be more than a side gig. It can grow into a business. It can grow into a blessing. A small seed that blossoms into financial freedom, community impact, and generational wealth.

Some people build wealth by selling products. Others make a fortune by selling possibilities. They offer services that solve problems, bring joy, and transform lives.

Serving with Vision

This is for the seamstress teaching young girls to sew, the caterer delivering home-cooked goodness at weddings, and the woman who chooses to share her knowledge rather than do the work. The truth is simple: you do not need a factory to build wealth. What truly matters is serving with vision and purpose.

The Wealth in Serving Others

There is something undeniably sacred about service. When you provide a service, whether it is braiding hair, baking cakes, coaching clients, or training others, you are doing more than earning a paycheck. You are:

- ❖ Sharing knowledge
- ❖ Multiplying your gifts
- ❖ Sparking transformation
- ❖ Adding emotional value

❖ Building trust and strengthening community

Service-based businesses may not always be flashy or loud, but they are deeply personal. They meet people exactly where they are. And because of that, they become powerful platforms for both Income and impact.

Three Service Paths to Prosperity

1. Fashion Schools: Teaching the Gift, Not Just Selling the Cloth

"Don't just wear the thread, teach others how to stitch their future."

Many talented designers dream of launching boutiques or fashion brands, and that is a beautiful goal. But what if your most significant impact—and Income came not from tailoring, but from teaching?

Running a fashion school or training center provides more than clothing. It delivers empowerment.

Why it works:

❖ **Scalable:** Train five students or fifty. Expand with digital courses, workshops, or bootcamps.

❖ **Low inventory costs:** Unlike a boutique, you do not need to keep fabric or finished goods in stock at all times.

❖ **High social impact:** You equip people with skills that can feed families and launch new businesses.

❖ **Recurring Income:** Students pay monthly or per session, providing a steady, reliable cash flow.

Emotional value: You are not just stitching fabric; you are weaving confidence into every student. You are also proving that knowledge is not meant to be hoarded; it is intended to be shared.

Story: Moremi Fashion Academy

The vision for Moremi Fashion Academy was born in 2015 when founder Moremi Victoria completed her first degree. Faced with the reality of high graduate unemployment in Nigeria, she thought deeply about her future. During her NYSC waiting period, she trained under uneducated local fashion professionals and discovered a troubling gap: apprenticeships were often unstructured, leaving many young people discouraged from learning.

After NYSC, she launched Moremi Fashion Store, focused on garment production. As the business grew, she realized her real value was in structured training. Within months, the store evolved into Moremi Fashion Academy, offering a full curriculum in design, business, and entrepreneurship.

Over the last seven years, the academy has trained more than 300 students, many of whom now work independently in the fashion industry. The academy expanded into consultancy to mentor new entrepreneurs and co-founded another brand, Moremi Photography and Cinematography Academy, with her husband, Mr. Folarin Johnson. What began as one woman's search for opportunity became a platform for hundreds to find empowerment, employment, and creativity.

2. Catering Services: Cooking for Purpose, Not Just Profit

"To feed someone is to enter their memory forever."

Food is a universal language. It unites, heals, celebrates, and comforts. If you have a gift for flavor, you hold a powerful key to building wealth.

Catering is not only about food. It is about creating unforgettable experiences. Weddings, birthdays, corporate events, and intimate family dinners all become richer because of the service you provide.

Why it works:

- ❖ **Low startup costs:** You can start with your kitchen, pots, and recipes.

- ❖ **High flexibility:** You decide when and how many orders to take.

26

- ❖ **Word-of-mouth power:** One excellent event can lead to multiple referrals.

- ❖ **Room for creativity:** You can design menus that reflect culture, health trends, or fusion concepts.

Emotional value: Cooking is sacred. Therefore, when you cater, you are not just filling plates. You are feeding souls. You are adding depth and meaning to life's most important celebrations.

Story: Emeka's Kitchen

Emeka lost his banking job but had a gift for cooking jollof rice that could "start a war." Instead of chasing another 9-to-5, he began accepting weekend catering orders. One wedding became two, then ten. Today, Emeka runs a catering business with eight staff and still stirs every pot himself. His secret was not just seasoning, it was passion.

3. Online Schools: Teaching in the Digital Age

Running a successful online school requires more than knowledge. It requires conviction. You are not just sharing information, you are changing lives.

You are:

- ❖ Helping someone reach a breakthrough.

- ❖ Making someone feel capable and seen.

- ❖ Assisting someone in rewriting their story.

- ❖ Equipping someone to earn, heal, or lead.

That is not just business. It is a call.

From Idea to Impact: Starting your Online School

You do not need expensive tools or a fancy website. Start purpose-driven and straightforward.

- ❖ **Choose your niche:** What do you love? What have you mastered or overcome?

- ❖ **Define transformation:** What result should your students achieve?

- ❖ **Select your format:** Pre-recorded video lessons, live Zoom classes, or email-based courses.

"Success is not just about starting. It is about growing."

Planting Seeds, Scaling Impact

You planted a seed of an idea. You watered it with effort, nurtured it with care, and kept showing up even when the harvest seemed far away.

The difference between those who merely get by and those who thrive comes down to one thing: scaling.

Thriving entrepreneurs do not just grind. They learn to work smarter. They expand their impact without burning out. They stop doing everything alone and start building systems, teams, and tools that allow the business to grow beyond their personal capacity.

Starting is a beautiful journey. But scaling? That is where transformation begins.

What Scaling Really Means

Scaling is about getting bigger. It is about becoming stronger and more sustainable. It is about growing Income, reach, and influence without multiplying stress.

It is a shift from:

- ❖ Surviving to building systems.

- ❖ Staying busy to become impactful.

- ❖ Doing everything alone to empower others.

Scaling looks like:

- ❖ Creating systems that function even when you are offline.
- ❖ Training a team to replicate your success.
- ❖ Automating repetitive tasks with technology.
- ❖ Expanding to new markets and audiences.

Scaling proves you have built something larger than yourself.

Overcoming the Fear of Scaling

Many people avoid scaling because of fear. They think, "No one can do it like me," or "What if the quality drops?" or "I am not ready."

But refusing to scale is like planting a seed and never letting it grow into a tree. Scaling is not about losing control. It is about building capacity and trusting your vision enough to allow others to carry it forward.

A scaled business is not only profitable; it is also sustainable. It becomes a force for good, a model for others, and a voice that carries even when you are absent.

Scaling as Inner Growth

Scaling is not just about hiring or automating. It is also a shift within you.

- ❖ Are you ready to step into leadership instead of worker mode?
- ❖ Are you willing to charge more because your value has grown?
- ❖ Are you prepared to stop carrying everything yourself?
- ❖ Are you ready to invest in systems, mentors, or support?

Scaling begins in the heart before it appears in the spreadsheets. It is the moment you realize that staying small does not serve anyone, not you, not your family, and not the people who need your solution.

You were not made to burn out in silence. You were built to create sustainable abundance.

An Inspiring Story of Scaling: From a Small Kitchen to the Global Table

Maria never set out to build an empire. She only wanted to share her grandmother's recipes with her community. With a borrowed stove and handwritten labels, she began selling spice blends and preserves at a neighborhood market.

Every jar carried more than flavor. It brought a story of culture, memory, and love.

As demand grew, Maria chose to treat her passion like a business. She reinvested every penny, listened to her customers, and built carefully. Her kitchen became a workshop, then a studio, and finally a full-scale operation employing women from her community.

Scaling for Maria wasn't only about producing more. It was about deepening purpose. She built systems that honored her values: sustainable sourcing, ethical labor, and storytelling. She partnered with chefs, wellness brands, and digital creators, taking her products global.

Today her products are found on tables from Lagos to London to Los Angeles. Yet she still keeps one jar from her very first batch as a reminder: growth never has to mean losing your soul.

Closing Thoughts

Money grows where you plant it. And service is one of the richest soils you can choose. Whether you are building a fashion academy, catering business, or online school, the principle remains the same: plant wisely, nurture consistently, and wait patiently.

Wealth is not magic. It is the natural result of seeds planted with vision, strategy, and courage.

Chapter 4

The Entrepreneurship Factor Creating Wealth Instead of Earning It

The Old Blueprint

Growing up, many of us were handed a clear blueprint for success: go to school, earn good grades, secure a stable job, and work hard until retirement. On the surface, this path promises security, respectability, and predictability.

And while it works for some, it also has limitations.

Earning a paycheck as an employee is honorable. But it often means surrendering control over your time, your Income, and even your long-term legacy.

Here's the truth: **real wealth is not just earned, it is created.** And one of the most potent ways to make it is through entrepreneurship.

What Entrepreneurship Really Means

Entrepreneurship is not simply about starting a business. It is about **creating value, solving problems, and building systems** that generate results even when you are not directly involved.

Think of it as planting seeds of your vision and watching them grow, not by hustling endlessly, but by scaling strategically and wisely.

From Employee to Entrepreneur: A Paradigm Shift

Let's explore the difference between earning a paycheck and creating lasting wealth.

The Employee Model:

- ❖ You trade time for money.
- ❖ Your Income is limited to the hours you put in.
- ❖ You operate within someone else's system.
- ❖ Security is present, but growth is capped.

The Entrepreneurial Model:

- ❖ You build income-generating systems that operate with or without you.
- ❖ You leverage time, people, and capital for exponential growth.
- ❖ Your Income is not tied to the clock.
- ❖ You own the work and the outcome.

Leaping from employee to entrepreneur can be terrifying. You step away from the illusion of security and into the unknown. There are risks, rejection, and responsibility.

But what you gain is far greater: freedom, ownership, and the opportunity to create a lasting legacy.

Leverage: The Secret Ingredient of Wealth Creation

Entrepreneurs do not build wealth by working harder. They make it by **leveraging resources** to multiply results. Economists call these increasing returns **to scale**.

Although previously explained, we can break down leverages and paint real-world examples as follows:

1. Time Leverage

Instead of trading hours for Income, entrepreneurs create systems that operate continuously.

Example: A Lagos baker, Tola, hit a ceiling baking cakes by hand. She later built an online course on cake decorating. Today, the course sells globally, generating Income even when she sleeps.

This is the power of time leverage—doing the work once and reaping the returns repeatedly.

2. People Leverage

Wise entrepreneurs recognize they cannot do everything alone. They hire, collaborate, and delegate. This is known in economics as **division of labor and specialization**, a principle that multiplies productivity.

Take Chuka, a tailor who began alone. As demand grew, he hired apprentices and later opened a small factory. Now, he focuses on branding and innovation while his team handles production.

That is people leveraging in action.

3. Capital Leverage

Money, when invested wisely, multiplies impact. Entrepreneurs reinvest profits, seek funding, or partner with investors to scale.

Consider Amina, a fashion designer. She secured a small business loan to open a storefront and hire staff. Within a year, her Income tripled. She didn't just work harder. She used **financial capital** to unlock growth.

The Emotional Landscape of Entrepreneurship

Entrepreneurship is not just about finances; it is about emotions. It demands resilience, adaptability, and vision.

❖ You will doubt yourself, especially at the beginning. **Impostor syndrome** is real, but so is your potential.

❖ You will face failure. Not every idea will succeed, but every failure offers a lesson.

❖ You need support. Mentors, peers, and communities create the ecosystem that sustains entrepreneurs.

Economists often speak of the **entrepreneurial ecosystem**, the networks, capital, and culture that determine whether businesses thrive or fail. On a personal level, your "ecosystem" is the people and habits you build around yourself.

Scaling: The Heart of Entrepreneurship

Scaling begins long before spreadsheets and profit margins. It starts with vision, the realization that staying small does not serve you, your family, or the people who need your solution.

Entrepreneurs do not just create businesses. They create **systems of abundance** that outlast them.

Take Maria, who started cooking in a tiny kitchen. With persistence, she grew her side hustle into a global spice-and-preserve brand. She reinvested profits, scaled intentionally, and created jobs for women in her community. Today, her products are sold from Lagos to London.

This is the essence of scaling: building systems that align with purpose, values, and long-term wealth.

Closing Thought

Entrepreneurship is the shift from earning a living to **creating wealth**. It transforms ideas into Income, labor into leverage, and vision into legacy.

When you embrace entrepreneurship, you stop living only for today's paycheck and start building tomorrow's prosperity.

Chapter 5

The Illusion of Financial Luck: Knowledge Beats Random Success

The Mirage of Overnight Success

We are all a little captivated by the idea of *overnight success*. One scroll through social media shows highlights reels of people flaunting luxury cars, exotic vacations, and stunning homes.

To the casual observer, it seems like luck is the magic key to financial freedom. A lottery win, a viral post, or one lucky break is all it takes— or so it appears.

But look closer. Beneath the shiny surface of sudden wealth lies a hard truth: **luck might hand you money, but only wisdom can help you keep it.**

Money Magnifies Who You Already Are

Here's the reality: money does not change you; it amplifies you.

- ❖ Without discipline, money fuels overspending and indulgence.
- ❖ With fear, it becomes a source of anxiety.
- ❖ Without direction, it invites chaos.

This is why so many lottery winners and overnight celebrities go broke within a few years. Behavioral economists call this **sudden wealth syndrome**, a state where money outpaces mindset.

True wealth is not about a random jackpot. It is about an opportunity to attend a preparation meeting. What looks like luck from the outside is often the result of **research, planning, and strategic action**.

Beyond Luck: The Power of Preparedness

Some people appear "lucky" because they invested in the right stock at the right time or launched a business just before the market shifted. But behind that timing is usually knowledge.

Economists call this **information asymmetry;** those with the right insights act earlier and reap greater rewards. To the uninformed, it looks like luck. To the informed, it is simply preparation.

Building Wealth Through Knowledge

1. Financial Education

Lasting wealth requires more than saving or budgeting. It begins with financial literacy—understanding money as a resource to cultivate and multiply.

Budgeting is not about restriction; it is about clarity and control. Tracking your Income, expenses, and savings gives you the **data** to make informed choices.

Not all debt is bad. Economists distinguish between **productive debt** (loans that fund businesses or assets) and **consumptive debt** (borrowing for lifestyle expenses). Knowing the difference can determine whether debt enriches you or enslaves you.

Investing, on the other hand, is how you put money to work—through stocks, bonds, mutual funds, or businesses—so that it grows even when you sleep.

2. Risk Management and Insurance

Wealth is not just about what you make but what you keep. One unexpected event shouldn't wipe out years of progress.

That's where risk management comes in. Insurance—health, life, property, and liability—is not just paperwork. It is an economic safety net. It protects your wealth from shocks that derail unprepared households.

3. Tax Planning and Legal Structures

Preserving wealth requires understanding the impact of taxation. Many wealthy individuals legally minimize their taxes through efficient structures such as trusts, wills, and business entities.

For entrepreneurs, proper registration not only ensures compliance but also allows access to incentives, contracts, and financing. In macroeconomic terms, tax literacy increases both personal prosperity and government revenue stability.

4. Legacy Planning

Money is a tool, not the ultimate goal. Legacy planning ensures your wealth outlives you and serves those you love.

This is not just about writing a will. It is about building generational systems: family businesses, education funds, land, or intellectual property. In Nigerian culture and the diaspora, legacy often defines whether families remain wealthy across generations—or fall back into poverty after one prosperous life.

Closing Thought

Luck is unpredictable. But knowledge, discipline, and strategy are dependable.

Financial literacy, risk management, tax efficiency, and legacy planning form the real foundation of wealth. These are not glamorous habits, but they create results that last longer than any lottery ticket or viral moment.

So, the next time you envy someone's "lucky break," remember that what looks like luck is often just a preparation meeting opportunity.

Chapter 6

Breaking the Money Myths: Practical Steps to Build Wealth

The Lies We Have Been Told

From childhood, many of us absorb beliefs about money through family, culture, and community. Sadly, some of these myths sabotage our financial growth before we even realize it. It is time to dispel those falsehoods and replace them with truths that empower.

Let's debunk the most pervasive myths:

Lie #1: "Money is the root of all evil."

Truth:

It is *the love of money* that invites trouble. Money itself is neutral. In the right hands, it funds schools, empowers entrepreneurs, and transforms communities. Economically speaking, it is simply a **medium of exchange,** neither good nor bad.

Lie #2: "There's never enough."

Truth:

Scarcity is more of a mindset than a reality. Our economy is dynamic and growing. Thanks to **positive-sum growth**, innovation and entrepreneurship keep expanding what's possible. When you adopt an abundance mindset, opportunities appear.

Lie #3: "Only the rich get richer."

Truth:

While systemic inequality exists, wealth is not an exclusive club. Many wealthy individuals began with nothing but vision, persistence, and discipline. Microeconomic theory shows that consistent, intentional action—such as reinvesting earnings and compounding over time produces upward mobility.

Lie #4: "You must work harder to earn more."

Truth:

While hard work is noble, innovative work—leveraging technology, systems, and networks—lets you do more with less. In business, that aligns with **economies of scale**: as you grow smarter, each unit of effort returns more.

Step One: Shift to a Growth Mindset

Scarcity whispers, "I'll never have enough." A growth mindset counters: "I can learn and grow."

- ❖ Identify financial beliefs that hold you back.
- ❖ Replace them with empowering truths.
- ❖ Reinforce your new beliefs daily for 21 days to reshape your mindset.

Step Two: Create Multiple Income Streams

Income diversification is a classic economic strategy for stability.

- ❖ **Active Income**—earned from jobs or freelancing.
- ❖ **Passive Income**—flows without daily effort (rent, royalties, online courses).
- ❖ **Portfolio Income**—returns from investments like stocks, bonds, and funds.

Balanced portfolios reduce risk and open doors to growth.

Step Three: Master Practical Financial Habits

You do not need to be a Wall Street expert. You need clarity, discipline, and consistency.

❖ Budget for control, not restriction.

❖ Save for security. Invest for growth.

❖ Distinguish **productive debt** (funding assets) from **consumptive debt** (instant gratification).

❖ Stay consistent—small steps, repeated over time, compound into life-changing results.

Step Four: Invest Smart — Portfolio Examples for Nigerians at Home and Abroad

Here are accessible, practical investment vehicles tailored to both Nigerian residents and diaspora investors:

A. Index Funds and ETFs in Nigeria

These are passive, low-cost funds that mimic market indices.

❖ **Stanbic IBTC ETF 30** tracks the NGX 30, providing diversified exposure to Nigeria's largest companies.

❖ **Vetiva Griffin 30**, **NGX Oil & Gas**, **NGX Pension**, and **NGX Industrial** are other index-tracking ETFs offering sector exposure.

❖ Notable performers in 2025 included the **Vetiva S&P Nigeria Sovereign Bond ETF** (up ~51% year-to-date), **Vetiva Consumer Goods ETF** (up ~46%), and the **NewGold ETF** tracking gold (up ~30%).

B. Mutual Funds in Nigeria

Managed by professionals, these funds pool capital to invest across asset classes.

- ❖ **Stanbic IBTC Aggressive Fund** — 90% equity exposure, returned ~49.9% in 2023.

- ❖ **ARM Ethical Fund** (Sharia-compliant) returned ~30.9% in Q1 2024.

- ❖ **ARM Fixed Income Fund** — offers stable yields of 12–15% from bonds.

- ❖ **Chapel Hill Denham Nigeria Dollar Income Fund** — dollar-denominated, protects against naira volatility.

- ❖ **Halo Equity Fund** — achieved over 100% returns year-to-date by early 2025 (high risk, high reward).

- ❖ **Alpha Morgan Balanced Fund** — blends equities and fixed Income for steadier growth.

- ❖ **GT Equity Income Fund** — combines dividends and bonds for Income and capital appreciation (~13% return).

C. Money Market Funds

Low risk and often outperform regular savings accounts.

Examples include **Cowrywise TrustBanc**, **United Capital**, **ARM Money Market**, and **Stanbic IBTC Money Market Fund**. Many of these have yielded around 20% annually.

D. Diaspora-Friendly Investing

Nigerians abroad can also tap into these opportunities.

- ❖ Top managers like **Stanbic IBTC**, **ARM**, **FBNQuest**, **Meristem**, and **Chapel Hill Denham** provide online platforms accessible to diaspora investors.

❖ These funds enable remote account setup, currency diversification, and professional management—all without being physically present in Nigeria.

Closing Thought

Financial myths keep us stuck. But when you replace false narratives with empowering truths, adopt a growth mindset, build diversified income channels, and invest via tools like index funds, ETFs, and mutual funds, you set yourself free.

Wealth grows where you plant it. Now, you have the garden layout. All that's left is to get planting. Let's watch that garden flourish together.

About The Author

Samson Osunkojo is a dynamic entrepreneur, visionary leader, and dedicated community builder. He is a proud member of the **African Young Entrepreneurs Network Initiative**, an organization committed to empowering and connecting young African business owners to scale their ventures to global standards.

As the CEO of **Goldenfield Investment Limited** and **ROB Investment**, Samson has built thriving enterprises in **real estate, agribusiness, and finance**. With over a decade of experience in **investment banking** and **business development**, he brings deep insights into wealth creation—expertise that inspired his book *Money Grows Where You Plant It*.

Guided by a philanthropic heart, Samson founded **Eyes on Talents Hub**, a foundation dedicated to uncovering hidden potential and launching it onto the world stage. He also established the **Omo Ibadan Heritage Club** and is a Board Member of Ibadan Youths Indigene. This socio-cultural association unites illustrious sons and daughters of Ibadan worldwide.

A passionate public speaker and mentor, Samson blends his entrepreneurial acumen with a commitment to education, community development, and youth empowerment.

He is happily married to his beloved wife, **Queen Opeyemi**, and together they are blessed with three sons and three adopted daughters.

www.ingramcontent.com/pod-product-compliance
Lightning Source LLC
Chambersburg PA
CBHW040931210326
41597CB00030B/5258